Broken But Beautiful

31 Day Devotional for Grieving Families

Marquisse Watson

Foreword by Antwon Watson

ROYSTON Publishing

BK Royston Publishing
P. O. Box 4321
Jeffersonville, IN 47131
502-802-5385
http://www.bkroystonpublishing.com
bkroystonpublishing@gmail.com

© Copyright – 2019

All Rights Reserved. No part of this book may be reproduced, stored in a retrieval system, or transmitted by any means without the written permission of the author.

Cover Layout: Gad Savage – Elite Covers
Photocredit Back Cover: KiKi Smith with KiKi Smith Photography
Photocredit Cover: Jason and Jordan Lindle

ISBN-13: 978-1-946111-84-5

Printed in the United States of America

Thank You

I would first like to thank God for giving me the strength and courage to write this book. I would like to thank my family and friends for all of your support, prayers, and encouragement over the years. And last but not least, I would like to thank my husband and my children. Thank you for being my biggest fans and believing in me, even when I didn't believe in myself!

In Loving Memory of Alana Marie Watson

May 22, 2014-May 23, 2014

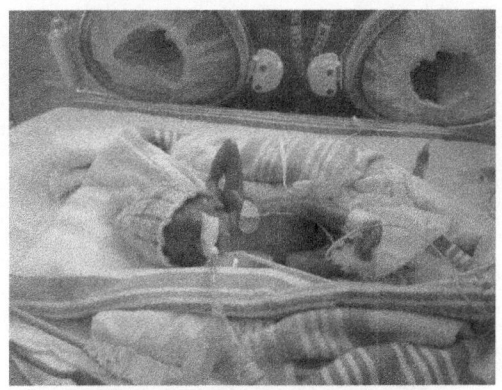

"And though she be but little, she is fierce." William Shakespeare

To learn more about The Alana Marie Project visit:
https://thealanamarieproject.com/

Table of Contents

Thank you		iii
In Loving Memory		v
Foreword		ix
Introduction		xi
Day 1	The Initial Shock	1
Day 2	Going Home Empty Handed	3
Day 3	In a Dark Place	5
Day 4	The First Sunday	7
Day 5	The Dreaded Postpartum Changes	9
Day 6	Planning the Final Arrangements	11
Day 7	The Call	13
Day 8	Feeling Hopeless	15
Day 9	I Can't Make it On My Own	17
Day 10	Coping	19
Day 11	Going Back to Work	21
Day 12	Dry Bones	23

Day 13	Supporting Your Spouse	25
Day 14	Your Due Date	27
Day 15	Triggers	29
Day 16	The Waiting Period	31
Day 17	The Holidays	33
Day 18	Faith Over Fear	35
Day 19	Forgiving Yourself	37
Day 20	Anniversary of Loss	39
Day 21	Rainbow Baby	41
Day 22	You Are Strong	43
Day 23	It's Okay to Be Okay	45
Day 24	The Depth of Love	47
Day 25	He's Able	49
Day 26	With God All Things Are Possible	51
Day 27	Pain Into Purpose	53
Day 28	Beauty For Ashes	55
Day 29	Your Story	57
Day 30	Leaving A Legacy	59
Day 31	Keep On Climbing	61

Foreword by Antwon Watson

A wise man once told me that there is healing in helping others heal. My wife, Marquisse Watson, has been able to capture the most difficult experience in our life and turn it into something beautiful. While in the storm, we were unable to see how any good could come from the pain of losing our firstborn, but were often reminded to trust God because he had a plan. God used our brokenness for a greater purpose. That purpose is to help families around the world whose stories are similar to ours.

Isaiah 61:3 says, "To all who mourn in Israel, he will give a crown of beauty for ashes, a joyous blessing instead of mourning, festive praise instead of despair. In their righteousness, they will be like great oaks that the Lord has planted for his own glory."

This book will bless the broken and help the hopeless find hope in the one from whom our strength comes, Jesus Christ. I pray that this 31-day devotional will help you find peace in your situation and know that God has a plan for you.

Antwon Watson

Co-founder of The Alana Marie Project

Introduction

Broken but beautiful sounds like a bit of an oxymoron. How can something broken be beautiful? This 31-day devotional will share how my husband and I, with God's help, turned a broken situation into something beautiful. I pray that this book brings hope to the hopeless and encourages the discouraged.

BROKEN

BUT

BEAUTIFUL

Day 1

The Initial Shock

"So do not fear, for I am with you; do not be dismayed (shocked), for I am your God. I will strengthen you and help you; I will uphold you with my righteous hand."
Isaiah 41:10

May of 2014 was full of many unexpected events that I couldn't believe were really happening. What started off as gestational hypertension turned into severe preeclampsia, which led me to being induced into labor at 24 weeks. When the doctors came in to tell me that I must be induced because my health was at risk, I felt in a complete state of shock. How could I deliver our baby girl at only 24 weeks?

Despite being given less than a 10% chance to survive the delivery, our daughter, Alana Marie Watson, was born at 24 weeks on May 22, 2014. Due to complications of her premature birth, Alana passed away on May 23, 2014.

Talk about being in a state of shock. The time between being admitted to the hospital for monitoring and the evening Alana passed away went so fast that I didn't even have time to process everything that happened.

Maybe you can relate to my story? The series of events leading to your loss may be similar to my story, or they may be completely different. Maybe you still feel like you are in a state of shock. Even though you may feel shocked and surprised by everything, remember there are no surprises to God.

Prayer:

Dear Lord,

I feel like I am in a state of shock. I can't believe or even wrap my mind around the series of events that led up to my loss. Your word tells me not to be dismayed or shocked, but if I'm honest — that's easier said than done. Strengthen me and help me to deal with the shock I am feeling.

In Jesus' name,

Amen

Day 2

Going Home Empty-Handed

"The Lord is close to the brokenhearted and saves those who are crushed in spirit."
Psalm 34:18

The day after Alana passed away, I wanted nothing more than to be discharged from the hospital. I literally couldn't stand the thought of being in the mother baby unit another day. I was a mother there without my baby. Hearing those precious cries was a painful reminder of something I never got to experience — hearing Alana cry.

I never expected to leave the hospital empty-handed without our baby girl. We left the hospital with a keepsake box of Alana's personal items, a pink **balloon** that said "Baby Girl," and our broken hearts.

Losing a baby, whether from miscarriage, stillbirth, or infant death, has a way of leaving even the strongest people feeling brokenhearted.

Prayer:

Dear Lord,

I feel so broken. It feels like my hopes and dreams of being a parent have been shattered before my very eyes. Help me to feel you near to me — the brokenhearted.

In Jesus' name,

Amen

Day 3

In a Dark Place

"Even though I walk through the darkest valley, I will fear no evil, for you are with me; your rod and your staff, they comfort me."

Psalm 23:4

On Saturday, May 24, 2014, we were finally discharged from the hospital. We stopped to grab a bite to eat and pick up some dry cleaning that I had dropped off prior to being admitted to the hospital. In my mind, it felt like we were taking the "walk of shame" — coming home from the hospital without Alana.

The first place I went when we got home was Alana's room. We had already painted her room, put together her crib, and filled her closet with the cutest clothes. When I walked into her room, I literally felt like I couldn't stand anymore. I lowered myself to the floor and just cried. All of the horrible events that had happened flashed before my eyes. Reality hit me. I wasn't just having a terrible nightmare — we really had just experienced the tragedy of losing our baby girl.

Talk about being in a dark place. When you got home from the hospital, where did you go first? Maybe you weren't able to walk in or even walk past your baby's room.

Prayer:

Dear Lord,

I am walking through the darkest valley. I don't see a light at the end of the tunnel. Comfort me.

In Jesus' name,

Amen

Day 4

The First Sunday

"Brothers and sisters, pray for us."
1 Thessalonians 5:25

The first Sunday after Alana passed away, my husband asked if I felt up to going to church. I didn't really feel up to it, but I knew that my spirit needed to go. **We were in a time of need. We were in need of prayer and support from our blood family and our church family.**

I spent most of the service in tears. I don't really remember any of the songs that were sung, or the sermon that was preached. But I do remember that our entire church prayed for us at the end of the service. There were no words to describe the feeling of hundreds of people praying for us. Those prayers along with the prayers of family and friends carried us through.

After the church prayed for us, a couple came up to my husband and I, introduced themselves, shared their story of losing a baby, and prayed with us.

Seeing a couple who had personally experienced a loss being able to share their story and encourage us gave me a glimpse of hope for our situation.

Maybe you don't have anyone to lean on for prayer or feel too far from God. There is still hope. God is right there to help you in your time of need.

Prayer:

Dear Lord,

I am approaching your throne asking you to help me in my time of need. Thank you for the prayers of family and friends. Thank you for placing people in my life that will pray for me when I don't feel strong enough to pray for myself.

In Jesus' name,

Amen

Day 5

The Dreaded Postpartum Changes

"But I will restore you to health and heal your wounds..."
Jeremiah 30:17

That Sunday afternoon after church we invited a few friends and family members over for a grill out. I know it seems a little crazy that we were hosting a grill out two days after Alana passed away, but we wanted to be surrounded by family and friends. We wanted to do something to take our minds off of the overwhelming sadness.

A few hours into the grill out, after playing a few games of spades, I called it a night. I said my goodbyes to everyone and went to lie in bed. I was physically and emotionally drained. The 37 hours of labor, recovering from severe preeclampsia, and postpartum changes finally caught up to me. I'm not sure which was the worst — the back pain from the epidural site, the cramping, or the swelling in my legs and feet.

One of the hardest things for me was that my body experienced so much pain and trauma, but I felt like I had nothing to show for it. Even if your baby passes away, your body must still go through the dreaded postpartum changes. What signs are your body showing that mean you need to rest?

Prayer:

Dear Lord,

My body has experienced many physical changes starting with the pregnancy and now in the postpartum phase. Restore my health. Help me to handle these changes and listen to my body's way of telling me to rest.

In Jesus' name,

Amen

Day 6

Planning The Final Arrangements

"For what is your life? It is but a vapor that appears for a little time and then vanishes away."

James 4:14

The week after Alana's passing, we received a call from the hospital to discuss final arrangements for Alana. Before we left the hospital, we were given some materials to review and contact information for a local funeral home. After the phone call ended, I knew we needed to take the next step — calling the funeral home. We set up a meeting at the funeral home later that week.

My husband and I both agreed that we didn't want a traditional funeral service. We just wanted this time to ourselves. The staff at the funeral home were very kind and helpful with explaining the options. After reviewing all of the options, we decided to have Alana cremated.

Prayer:

Dear Lord,

I never imagined I would be making final arrangements for my baby. This is such a reminder that life is but a vapor. Help me to cherish the time I have left with my family and friends.

In Jesus' name,

Amen

Day 7

The Call

"To be absent from the body and to be present with the Lord."
2 Corinthians 5:8

Over the next several days, we received multiple phone calls from the funeral home. The first call notified us that Alana had been picked up from the hospital and taken to the funeral home. Another call was to let us know that Alana was being taken to the crematorium. And a final call was to let us know that Alana's cremains were ready for us to pick up.

I am so thankful for that funeral home. They treated us with such dignity and respect. Even though our baby had passed away, they referred to her by name and kept us informed throughout the entire process. The ride to and from the funeral home to pick up Alana's cremains was a difficult one. I don't remember exchanging many words, but the tears were almost too many to count.

And, finally, our baby girl was home. Not the way we had hoped, but we were finally able to bring Alana home.

Prayer:

Dear Lord,

I know that to be absent from the body is to be present with you. My baby is with you in a place with no pain or worries. I want to live my life so that I can make it to that place someday.

In Jesus' name,

Amen

Day 8

Feeling Hopeless

"Come to me all who are weary and burdened and I will give you rest."
Matthew 11:28

Have you ever been in a situation where you felt weary, burdened, and hopeless? I was certainly at that place after Alana passed away. My husband, Antwon, was not given much time off work after Alana's death. After he went back to work, I was home alone a lot during the day.

Grief and mourning often lead to a place of isolation. It is okay to want some alone time, but being alone too much can leave a lot of time for your mind to wander down dark paths.

Family and friends would stop by to check on me, but some days I just wanted to be alone. My emotions were all over the place. It seemed like I would bounce between sad, sadder, and saddest.

None of my clothes fit, which didn't help the situation. The only way I could think to deal with the hopeless feeling was to eat. I turned to food for comfort. I would eat because I was sad, and I would get sad because I was eating too much and gaining weight.

Prayer:

Dear Lord,

I feel so hopeless. I am coming to you weary and burdened. I give you my burdens in exchange for your rest.

In Jesus' name,

Amen

Day 9

I Can't Make It On My Own

"By myself I can do nothing..."
John 5:30

Before Alana was born, I would have rated my spiritual life a 5 out of 10. I was a Christian; I had accepted Jesus into my heart as a teenager. Antwon and I attended church most Sundays. But I can't say that I put much effort into my relationship with God outside of church.

From the time I found out the severity of Alana's situation, I prayed harder than I had prayed in a long time. Isn't it terrible that we wait until we are in a bad situation to double up on praying? It wasn't until I had my world flipped upside down that I realized I couldn't make it on my own.

Losing Alana knocked me to my knees physically and spiritually. If I was going to make it through that storm, I knew I needed to rely on God to carry me to the other side.

How would you rate your walk with God? What can you do to improve your faith walk?

Prayer:

Dear Lord,

Forgive me for neglecting my relationship with you. Even when I neglected my relationship with you, you were still right there for me. Thank you for being there to carry me through this storm.

In Jesus' name,

Amen

Day 10

Coping

"Blessed are those who mourn, for they will be comforted."
Matthew 5:4

Having six weeks off work after Alana passed away left with me a lot of free time. I knew I needed to find something to do to keep me busy and keep my mind occupied.

One morning while I was watching TV, I tuned in to a sermon by one of my favorite preachers. I don't remember the exact title of the sermon, but it seemed like he was speaking directly to me and my situation. After listening to that sermon, I ordered a 31-day audio devotional series from that pastor. I looked forward to hearing each day's message from that devotional. Every time I listened to it, I felt a little stronger.

Another thing that really helped me cope was pulling out my creative side. I went to a few craft stores one afternoon. I filled my cart with stickers, decals, encouraging mementos, glue, and the cutest pink scrapbook. When I got home, I worked for hours creating a scrapbook for Alana. I wanted to capture her story so she would never be forgotten.

What are your ways for coping? Maybe you are good at sewing, writing, or crafting? Finding an activity that you enjoy can be a great outlet throughout the grief process.

Prayer:

Dear Lord,

I am in a season of mourning. Comfort me. Help me to find therapeutic ways to cope and to process the emotions I am feeling.

In Jesus' name,

Amen

Day 11

Going Back to Work

"Have I not commanded you? Be strong and courageous..."
Joshua 1:9

The six weeks off work seemed to fly by. Before I realized it, it was the night before my first day back to work. I had a mix of emotions. I was happy to get back into a normal routine, but I was also nervous. Nervous of what people would say, nervous of how my first day back would go. The last place I was pregnant before going to the hospital was work, so that also made me nervous.

My coworkers were all very supportive and welcoming on my first day back. The charge nurse gave me a light patient assignment so that I could ease back into being at work. My morning was off to a great start; I was on my way to give medications to one of my patients when the worst thing happened.

A doctor stopped me in the hallway and said he hadn't seen me in a while. I simply replied, "I had some time off." He looked at my belly, which was back to normal, and said "You had the baby, congrats." Immediately my eyes filled with tears, and I replied, "She passed away." At that moment I wanted to crawl into a shell and hide.

Have you gone back to work yet? How was your first day? If you haven't gone back to work yet, what are you dreading the most?

Prayer:

Dear Lord,

Going back to work after losing my baby was harder than I expected. Give me strength and courage. Help me to handle any situation that may arise after my return.

In Jesus' name,

Amen

Day 12
Dry Bones

"Son of man, can these bones live?"
Ezekiel 37:3

Before going back to work, I felt like I was finally getting a handle on my emotions. But going back to work pulled a lot of emotions to the surface — some I didn't even realize were there. I quickly realized it was hard to take care of sick people, when my heart was still so sick. Every night before work I would feel sick and anxious. I would often cry on my way to work because I didn't feel strong enough to handle the stress of another day taking care of patients.

I was hurting and found it very hard to show compassion to my patients. I found myself filled with negative thoughts about how terrible my job was, which led to a lack of patience. The once compassionate nurse had turned into an old grump. I didn't like the nurse I was becoming, which led me to pursue a new job and leave bedside nursing.

Have you experienced emotions such as anger that you didn't realize you were facing? How did those emotions come to the surface?

Prayer:

Dear Lord,

I feel like a pile of dry bones. I don't like this feeling. Bring my dry bones back to life again.

In Jesus' name,

Amen

Day 13

Supporting Your Spouse

"It always protects, always trusts, always hopes, always perseveres. Love never fails."

1 Corinthians 13:7-8

Before Alana passed away, I don't think I had ever seen my husband cry. The evening Alana passed away, I witnessed him crying for the first time. He probably hadn't cried since his grandmother passed away years earlier. Seeing him cry hurt my heart even more. Since Antwon didn't get much time off work after Alana's passing, he didn't really get much time to grieve. Antwon was getting back into his normal routine and seemed to be handling everything pretty well.

It wasn't until years later that Antwon really opened up to me about his perspectives on our loss. He confessed he didn't want to discuss being sad or missing Alana with me because he didn't want to make me upset or emotional.

Men and women handle grief differently. Women tend to be more open about their feelings. And men tend to be more stoic. Many times, the grieving mother is offered more support and counsel, but grieving fathers need support too.

What can you do to support your spouse during this difficult time?

Prayer:

Dear Lord,

Thank you for giving me my spouse to walk with me on this journey of loss. A situation like losing a baby can either make or break a marriage. Let this storm strengthen our relationship. Help our love and bond grow stronger than ever before.

In Jesus' name,

Amen

Day 14

Your Due Date

"There is a time for everything and a season for every activity under heaven."

Ecclesiastes 3:1

Before I realized it, the summer of 2014 was coming to an end. We were nearing Labor Day, our one-year wedding anniversary, and Alana's due date. The closer we got to September 8, the harder it was. When I first found out my due date would be the day after our first wedding anniversary, I was so excited. I envisioned that we would have a nice dinner to celebrate our wedding anniversary and then I would go into labor later that night. Sounds perfect, right?

I never imagined that we would be celebrating our first anniversary as grieving parents. It was hard to be excited about celebrating our wedding anniversary, when the next day was the day I had dreamed of ever since our first ultrasound — our due date. It was a reminder of a dream shattered.

Prayer:

Dear Lord,

I know there is a time and a season for everything. If I'm honest, this season is by far the hardest. Please be with me during this difficult season.

In Jesus' name,

Amen

Day 15

Triggers

"Recalling your tears, I long to see you, so that I may be filled with joy."

2 Timothy 1:4

If I could choose one thing to be warned about regarding the grief process, I would choose triggers. Handling triggers can be rough. Some triggers are obvious, and others not so much.

It seemed as if every woman in the world became noticeably pregnant after we lost Alana. Honestly, when I saw another pregnant woman, I would get jealous, sad, and a little mad. If only I could have stayed pregnant a little longer, maybe Alana would still be alive. Even something like a "normal" trip to Target became a little overwhelming. Walking past any baby-related items would lead to tears.

One of the not-so-obvious triggers was when Antwon sent me a picture of the produce setup at his job, and I saw blueberries. It reminded me when Alana was as tiny as a blueberry (according to the pregnancy app I used). Seeing pickles in the grocery store or at a restaurant would bring flashbacks of the crazy pickle cravings I had when pregnant with Alana. There were so many things that reminded me, and still remind me, of Alana.

What triggers have you identified? Do those triggers remind you of happy or sad memories?

Prayer:

Dear Lord,

I didn't realize all of the things that would trigger my emotions. Some trigger happy thoughts of my pregnancy, but others trigger sadness and tears. Help me to deal with the triggers I am facing.

In Jesus' name,

Amen

Day 16

The Waiting Period

"After he had patiently endured, he obtained the promise."
Hebrews 6:15

Have you ever wanted something so much that it consumed all of your thoughts? Well, that's how we felt about becoming parents again. Because of the rapid and early onset of preeclampsia, my obstetrician (OB) felt it would be best to see a high-risk maternal fetal medicine (MFM) doctor and get clearance to try again. I scheduled my appointment and counted down the days to meet the doctor.

I was a little nervous about seeing the MFM doctor, but I knew I needed to see her to get the necessary follow-up recommendations and expertise. At my appointment, the doctor voiced her concern and recommended follow-up testing that I should have done. She told us if all of the tests came back normal, we could start trying. We had waited so long to hear those words!

Antwon and I were so excited about the possibility of becoming parents again. We anxiously awaited the month we would get a positive pregnancy test. After a few months of trying, on December 9, 2014, our prayers were answered. We were pregnant again! Our journey to becoming parents again had begun.

Are you in a period of waiting? Maybe you and your spouse have decided it's time to try again. What are your concerns about a future pregnancy?

Prayer:

Dear Lord,

Please be with me during this time of waiting. Give me patience as we go from month to month waiting for a positive pregnancy test. I know our time is coming!

In Jesus' name,

Amen

Day 17

The Holidays

"And he will be called wonderful counselor, mighty God, everlasting father, prince of peace."
Isaiah 9:6

Before I realized it, the holiday season was in full swing. Antwon and I decided to keep the pregnancy a secret until after the holidays. As much as I wanted to be excited, I just couldn't get into the holiday spirit. We found ways to include Alana in our Christmas traditions. We found two ornaments — one a letter "A" and the other a heart with a poem — that we hung on our tree in her honor. We also chose to focus on giving instead of receiving and adopted a family as a way to give back.

Before Alana was born, I had already picked out the outfit she would wear on her first Christmas. I imagined a wonderful time spent with family and our new baby girl. Even though I enjoyed our Christmas with family that year, there was just something missing.

Holidays after a loss are tough. Everyone is full of Christmas cheer, but you are full of grief. You may not feel like attending the family gatherings or being in a jolly mood, and that's okay. What are some ways you plan to incorporate your angel baby into this holiday season?

Prayer:

Dear Lord,

I know the holidays are supposed to be a time of joy, but I feel quite the opposite. Help me to remember the true meaning of this holiday season — to celebrate the birth of our Lord and Savior Jesus Christ.

In Jesus' name,

Amen

Day 18

Faith Over Fear

"For God has not given us the spirit of fear; but of power, and of love, and of a sound mind."
2 Timothy 1:7

With the excitement of our news also came fear. The fear and anxiety almost became crippling. I was anxious because I was fearful. In my mind, I would think, "What if we lose this baby too? I can't imagine going through another loss." It was hard to enjoy the pregnancy because I was so fearful.

One Sunday our pastor preached an eye-opening message on fear. She mentioned that God has not given us the spirit of fear. She also emphasized that we can have faith or we can have fear — they can't coexist.

By the end of the sermon, I knew I needed to confront my fears. I decided I wasn't going to let fear control me anymore. I won't lie and say I was immediately set free from fear, but I was more aware of the fear and knew how to fight it — with God's word.

Whenever a fearful thought would come into my mind, I would fire back with God's word and promises.

Is fear trying to consume your life? What are your plans to deal with that fear?

Prayer:

Dear Lord,

I have been living in a fearful state since losing my baby. Fear of losing others, fear of experiencing another loss, and fear of the unknown. You didn't give me a spirit of fear, but of power, of love, and of a sound mind.

In Jesus' name,

Amen

Day 19

Forgiving Yourself

"Be kind and compassionate to one another, forgiving each other, just as in Christ God forgave you."
Ephesians 4:32

The cat was out of the bag when we shared our exciting news with the world at a dinner/gender-reveal party. We were excited to welcome a sweet baby boy to our family. The pregnancy was going well minus the morning (or all-day) sickness, until the headaches started. I knew from experience that the headaches meant high blood pressure.

When the high blood pressure started this time, I started to blame myself. What did I do wrong to end up with high blood pressure again? I started to feel guilty and beat myself up. Then my mind started telling me, "If I hadn't eaten so many pickles when I was pregnant with Alana, then I wouldn't have developed high blood pressure, and she would still be alive." I finally came to my senses and realized I did not cause the high blood pressure that led to preeclampsia. I had to forgive myself and be kind and compassionate with my thoughts to and about myself.

Have you been beating yourself up about your loss and holding a grudge against yourself? Now is the time to forgive yourself.

Prayer:

Dear Lord,

Why is it so easy to forgive others, but so hard to forgive myself? I will no longer blame myself for the complications that led to me losing my baby. I forgive myself and will treat myself with the same kindness and compassion that I show others.

In Jesus' name,

Amen

Day 20

Anniversary Of Loss

"You will keep in perfect peace those who minds are steadfast because they trust in you."
Isaiah 26:3

As much as I tried not to think about what was coming up, it happened. We were approaching the month of May. May used to be one of my favorite, most anticipated months, but this year I was dreading it. In May 2014, on my birthday, we found out that Alana was behind in her growth and development, and exactly two weeks later she was born.

How could an entire year have gone by so quickly? So much had changed over that year. I was not the same person I was in May 2014, and neither was Antwon. And now to think we were expecting our rainbow baby.

We weren't exactly sure what we wanted to do to celebrate Alana's birthday, but we knew we wanted to do something special. We started our day with an ultrasound to check on our baby boy — who was growing and doing very well. Then we had lunch with our family, followed by a balloon release. The next day was a rather quiet day, spent looking through pictures and Alana's keepsakes. I think Alana would have been pleased with the simple but special celebration in her honor.

How will you celebrate your baby's heavenly birthday?

Prayer:

Dear Lord,

I knew this month was coming, as much as I didn't want it to. Help me to stay in perfect peace during this time of honoring and remembering my baby. May this be a time to be surrounded by family.

In Jesus' name,

Amen

Day 21

Rainbow Baby

"Like the appearance of a rainbow in the clouds on a rainy day, so was the radiance around him."
Ezekiel 1:28

By the end of June 2015, at a little over 31 weeks, I had earned myself an admission ticket to the special care OB unit at a local hospital. My blood pressure was becoming harder to control, my legs and feet were extremely swollen, and I had increased protein in my urine. All of those are signs of preeclampsia.

I spent nearly two weeks in the hospital on bedrest. A typical day was spent laying on my left side, catching up on sleep, and anxiously waiting the day our baby boy would be born. Being in the hospital wasn't the most pleasant experience, but I knew it needed to be done to keep our baby safe. I did look forward to my trip to the ultrasound department to check on the baby's growth.

Right around 33 weeks, I started to show respiratory symptoms from the development of pulmonary edema and pleural effusions from the preeclampsia. On the evening of July 3, the induction process was started. After about 15 hours of labor on July 4, I gave birth to our rainbow baby, an adorable 4 lb. 2 oz. baby boy, Antwon Junior (AJ). And this time, I actually got to hold our baby before he was taken to the NICU. A dream that had been shattered a year earlier was fulfilled that day.

Prayer:

Dear Lord,

It didn't seem like this day would ever happen, but it's here. Thank you for blessing us with our rainbow baby. This baby is truly a sign that something beautiful can happen in the middle of the darkest storm.

In Jesus' name,

Amen

Day 22

You Are Strong

"But those who hope in the Lord shall renew their strength."
Isaiah 40:31

Antwon and my dad followed alongside AJ and the NICU team to the NICU. I couldn't wait until I had recovered enough to see AJ. Antwon and my dad were sure to send pictures and update me on AJ's progress. He didn't require any respiratory support, and he spent only a few hours in the closed incubator to help regulate his body temperature.

As excited as I was to go and visit AJ in the NICU, I was also nervous. I told myself a year prior that I could never step foot in that NICU again, but the time had come. Even though AJ's situation was much different than Alana's had been, it was still the same NICU. It was the place where I held Alana for the first and last time, and the place where we said our final goodbyes to her.

Two days after AJ was born, I was discharged from the hospital, but he was not. Even though I knew he would be coming home eventually, it was still overwhelmingly difficult to leave without him. I visited AJ in the NICU usually twice a day — once in the morning, and then Antwon and I would meet there in the evening. I remember crying so many times on my way home from the NICU because I was so ready to bring AJ home. After the longest 25 days, AJ was discharged from the NICU.

Prayer:

Dear Lord,

My body has been through so much physically and emotionally, and I don't feel strong. Help me to remember that true strength comes from you.

In Jesus' name,

Amen

Day 23

It's Okay To Be Happy

"Weeping may endure for a night, but joy comes in the morning."
Psalm 30:5

A new chapter in our life began when we brought AJ home from the hospital. We were finally together as a family. Bringing AJ home was a huge milestone, and we were so excited. Even though AJ was almost a month old, we felt like we were fish out of water on our first night at home with him.

For the past 25 days, we had had our security blanket — the NICU nurses who had been there to hold our hands and show us how to care for our baby boy. And now we were on our own. Our parenting instincts just seemed to kick in. About two weeks after AJ was discharged from the hospital, I returned to work. As much as I missed him while I was gone, it felt good to get back into a normal routine.

For the first time in a long time, I felt happy and content about our life. Watching AJ grow from month to month filled my heart with so much joy. But I found myself feeling guilty for being so happy and full of joy. How could I be so happy without Alana? I eventually realized it's okay to be happy again after losing your baby. It doesn't mean you forgot the pain of your loss, but you are thankful for the life and blessings you still have after the loss.

Are you experiencing feelings of guilt? It's okay to be happy again!

Prayer:

Dear Lord,

Thank you for this season of my life. It feels so good to have my joy back! I'm so thankful that you have allowed me to experience joy, despite the heartache I have faced. And I will not allow myself to feel guilty for being happy again.

In Jesus' name,

Amen

Day 24

The Depth Of Love

"Nothing can separate us from the love of God."
Romans 8:38-39

It seemed like losing Alana caused me to look at life very differently than I had before. After the initial grief process and withdrawal from family, I started to look forward to more family time. I yearned for spending quality time with Antwon and AJ. I didn't realize my heart was possible of loving someone as much as I loved Antwon and AJ. Becoming a mom brought out a new depth of love I had never experienced before.

And even though Alana isn't physically here with us, I've never stopped loving her. It seems that my love and appreciation for her have grown even stronger since her passing. Alana's life helped me find purpose in mine, and that makes me love and appreciate her even more.

Prayer:

Dear Lord,

Thank you for the reminder that nothing can separate us from your love. And even with my baby's death, nothing can separate the love I have for my baby. Thank you for loving me and allowing me to experience a love so deep.

In Jesus' name,

Amen

Day 25

He's Able

"Now to him who is able to do immeasurably more than all we can ask or imagine…"
Ephesians 3:20

Antwon and I were finally into the groove of parent life. AJ was on a good schedule and we felt like we had a handle on being parents. Then the unexpected happened. I woke one morning not feeling like myself and knew something was wrong. I took a pregnancy test, and it was positive! Talk about a complete shocker. AJ was about 9 months old when we found out we were expecting baby #3.

Finding out I was pregnant made me think of the quote, "We plan and God laughs." Up until this point Antwon and I weren't even sure we would have more children, especially with my track record for complicated pregnancies. Of course, I was very excited, but I was also nervous. "How will this pregnancy go? Can I even take care of two kids at the same time? Will AJ adjust to being a big brother?" Those were just a few questions that filled my mind.

How do you respond to the surprises of life?

Prayer:

Dear Lord,

I know nothing catches you by surprise. This moment was planned before I was even formed in my mother's womb. Lord, I trust the plan you have for my life. I know that your plan is far greater than what I can even ask or imagine.

In Jesus' name,

Amen

Day 26

With God All Things Are Possible

"With man this is impossible, but with God all things are possible."
Matthew 19:26

Since I had preeclampsia with my first two pregnancies, I was considered high risk and needed to be monitored very closely. I am very thankful for a wonderful OB/GYN who took such great care of me throughout the pregnancy.

Week after week went by. My blood pressure remained normal, there was no swelling, and my 24-hour urine tests were normal. It was unbelievable. Before I realized it, I had surpassed the 24-week mark when Alana was born and then the 33-week mark when AJ was born. I finally got to experience the part of pregnancy when you are really uncomfortable. After a completely uneventful pregnancy, at 39 weeks and 1 day, I gave birth to our first full-term baby, Andrew Watson. And 24 hours after he was born, we were discharged and went home together as a family. Talk about a miracle.

Is there a situation in your life that seems impossible? Remember with God all things are possible!

Prayer:

Dear Lord,

What seemed impossible in man's eyes is possible with you. Thank you for allowing me to experience a miracle firsthand. Thank you for giving me the desire of my heart — to experience a full-term pregnancy with no complications.

In Jesus' name,

Amen

Day 27

Pain Into Purpose

"And we know that in all things God works for the good of those who love him, who have been called according to his purpose."
Romans 8:28

From the moment Alana passed away, I knew God had a purpose for us to experience such a tragedy. Even though I couldn't see how, I knew that God would bring something good out of this situation. Within a few months of Alana passing away, whenever I would hear of another family who experienced the loss of a baby, I felt a tug on my heart to reach out and offer support and prayers.

From 2014 to 2018, I reached out to many families by sending sympathy cards and other items. But I felt a pull on my heart to do more and have a greater impact on grieving families.

At the end of 2017 and the beginning of 2018, I started talking to Antwon about what we could do to have a greater impact and serve even more families. In February 2018, I applied to start a nonprofit organization in the state of Ohio. On February 16, 2018, we officially started "The Alana Marie Project."

How can you channel your pain into purpose?

Prayer:

Dear Lord,

It is hard to wrap my mind around how you will bring something good out of this situation. I trust and believe that one day I will see a light in the darkness and how I can encourage others like me.

In Jesus' name,

Amen

Day 28

Beauty For Ashes

"To comfort all who mourn, and provide for those who grieve in Zion — to bestow on them a crown of beauty instead of ashes, the oil of joy instead of mourning, and a garment of praise instead of a spirit of despair."

Isaiah 61:2-3

Antwon and I knew nothing about starting or running a nonprofit. We just knew that God was calling us to have a greater impact. Starting The Alana Marie Project (TAMP) was a big leap of faith, but we trusted God!

Starting TAMP was our way of turning ashes into beauty. Antwon and I wanted to use our pain for a purpose by helping other families who have experienced the loss of a baby from miscarriage, stillbirth, or infant death. TAMP was created to encourage, empower, and support families like ours.

Since we started TAMP, God has shown himself faithful and guided us every step of the way. It is truly an honor to serve families in this capacity. Antwon and I have both found healing in helping others heal.

Prayer:

Dear Lord,

Your word says you will give me beauty for ashes, joy for mourning, and hope for despair. Thank you for these promises you have given me. Help me to recall this promise at a time when I need to be reminded the most.

In Jesus' name,

Amen

Day 29

Your Story

"They triumphed over him by the blood of the Lamb and by the word of their testimony..."
Revelation 12:11

Because of The Alana Marie Project, we have been able to share our story and reach even more families. We have been able to share how God will take a broken situation and bring something beautiful out of it. We have been able to share how God can and will restore joy even after the darkest night. We have been able to share how even though it felt like our life ended after Alana's passing, it was just the beginning of a "But God" story!

Sometimes it is still hard to share our story. Sometimes I can tell it without crying, but there are other times when I still shed tears, especially on parts of the story that are painful. And that's okay.

You are the only one who can share your story. When is the last time you shared your story with someone who needs to hear it? Maybe you have never shared your story with anyone. Maybe you are nervous, and that's okay. Sharing your story can be done with spoken words, written words, and/or pictures. You have a story that will encourage and inspire someone, so share it!

Prayer:

Dear Lord,

Give me the strength and courage to share my story. I know it may be tough — but that's okay. I know you will be there to help and strengthen me!

In Jesus' name,

Amen

Day 30

Leaving A Legacy

"In the same way, let your light shine before others, that they may see your good deeds and glorify your Father in Heaven."

Matthew 5:16

Alana's name and story have been shared more in her passing than during her short time here on earth. How is it possible that a tiny 15 oz. baby could make such an impact on others? Alana's life left behind a legacy of love and support.

The Alana Marie Project hopes to shine a light for families in a dark situation. For every family we are connected with, we pray that we can provide encouragement and an example of hope.

After Alana passed away, I promised myself that her life would not be forgotten. Every time I write The Alana Marie Project, I feel like a proud momma. Alana's life will continue to be a beacon of light and hope!

Prayer:

Dear Lord,

Out of this dark situation, help me to leave a legacy. I want to be a beacon of light and hope to families like mine. Place a family in my path that I can encourage and support. Let your light shine through me.

In Jesus' name,

Amen

Day 31

Keep On Climbing

> "I lift my eyes to the mountains — where does my help come from? My help comes from the Lord, the maker of heaven and earth."
>
> Psalm 121:1-2

After Alana first passed away, climbing this mountain of grief felt impossible and unbearable. It seemed I would never make it out of the valley. Some days it felt like I took five steps forward, and others days ten steps backwards. Some days the pain was unbearable, and I didn't feel like I could hold on any longer.

I wouldn't be where I am on this climb without God's help. Some days it felt like He literally carried me up parts of the mountain. He took over the parts of the journey I wasn't strong enough to climb.

Grief isn't something you will ever completely conquer. On days when you feel discouraged, look back down the mountain and see how far you have come. And while you are looking down, notice others who are climbing. Reach out your hand to help someone who has just started their climb or is hitting a rough patch on their journey.

Where are you on your grief journey? How can you help someone else along this climb?

Prayer:

Dear Lord,

Thank you for the reminder that I am not climbing this mountain alone. My help comes from you. You are with me every step of the way. Thank you for carrying me through the parts that were too hard for me to handle on my own.

In Jesus' name,

Amen

www.ingramcontent.com/pod-product-compliance
Lightning Source LLC
Chambersburg PA
CBHW031638160426
43196CB00006B/471